Quiet Flows the Hull

Clint Wastling

Stairwell Books //

Published by Stairwell Books
161 Lowther Street
York, YO31 7LZ

www.stairwellbooks.co.uk
@stairwellbooks

Quiet Flows the Hull © 2023 Clint Wastling and Stairwell Books

Layout design: Alan Gillott
Cover photograph: the author

ISBN: 978-1-913432-65-2
p6

Also by Clint Wastling

Novels
The Geology of Desire
Tyrants Rex

To Brenda for her love and encouragement,
also our children, grandchildren and friends.

Table of Contents

Receiver of Wreck

Lowest tide reveals
the boiler, back broken,
a reef of rust for barnacles,
substrate for a new ecosystem;
high pressure steam long forgotten.

Looking through the eyelet,
the ghost of a propeller
drives this schooner back
to a November fog
and funnel belching smoke.

Take a sounding!
Twenty five fathoms, sir!

After, sand parted, accommodating the hull
and *The Laura* turned from vessel
to vassal beneath cliffs of Speeton Clay.
Tug lines snagged, snapped.
Receiver of Wreck informed.

The cargo of coke salvaged.
The vessel salvaged,
boilers remain, rendered
by tides into a parody of pipes,
exposed to the sea. ⁄⁄

Hope

It could be a tedious task on a cold day –
direct traffic, ask people to remain
in their cars until five minutes before.
This freezing, sunny day in Brough was
vaccination day for the over 80s.

Same atmosphere as Christmas
but a gift with greater potential
for the only generation to remember The War.
They needed to get out for the first time.
It was dry, they could chat,

queue in the cold, not so much
feeling the need, hopefully feeling the needle.
Inside – hands, face, space, clipboards,
a one-way system out again.
Hope first time in a year.

Thankyous and goodbyes shared
with us carpark volunteers.
How the world has changed;
how quickly it changes for the better.
Being done. First step to a post-lockdown life. ⁄⁄

Susurration

I rest my weary head
and watch the sky,
forget my worries, listen,
breathe to the rhythm,
my finger held steady
charting direction in the push of clouds.

Sunlight chases the breeze
over a field of barley,
bending and releasing stems.
I take a video to remind me
how awns bristle
like insects on a summer evening.

Susurration of trees.
Each possesses a voice.
Blindfold in a forest,
I'd know the sound
of oak, ash, beech, willow –
silence under the hush of yew. ⁄⁄

Still Life with Skylark

Throughout these months of lockdown
we've heard skylarks. How their song
changes subtly as days lengthen.
At the beach we sit and read,
listening to gentle waves,
feeling the breeze wash over skin
scorched by midday sun.

From fields the skylark strikes up
a solo, staking its territory,
louder in the empty sky – invisible
but echoed by another more distant.
We've staked our territory
without singing, as tide turns,
as shadows lengthen.

Silence is broken by heartbeat of waves.
The Earth is alive! We are alive!
Paddling through warm salt-water,
thinking of those not with us:
rules relaxed but not enough –
not yet to fold our grandchild
into a warm summer embrace. ⁄⁄

Riding the Riding

Lockdown provides more time to cycle.
You feel part of the countryside,
embraced by it, higher on a saddle,
able to peer over hedgerows
at land we're forbidden to access.

Late spring – the colours are varied;
air scented with May and rapeseed;
verges alive with butterflies:
small white, orange tip, peacock, wall brown.

Cycling The Wolds from
High Hunsley to South Dalton.
A flask of coffee, bananas, biscuits,
for breaks on benches, watching
holly blue, tortoiseshell, brimstone yellow.

Fair-weather cyclists indulged by sun
on roads so quiet birdsong delights
and the soil smells damp from dew.
A landscape brimful under a sky of blue. ⁄⁄

Murmuration

thousands moving as one

biologists theorise
on a hive mind

does the same pattern happen in
their proteins and neurones

chemists remind us of
endorphins coursing

mathematicians describe
murmurations with equations
of critical transitions

physicists talk of systems
poised on the brink
of instantaneous transformations

reality is a hundred thousand starlings
moving as one

an avalanche of birds

one changes direction
all follow ⁄⁄

Folly Lake

People who lived on the land
were turfed off,
forbidden access,
fenced out.
The church demolished
to enhance Sir's view.

The rich don't change.
Public footpath –
bar the way.
Expensive barristers
employed,
so you don't get justice.
Land is stolen
from us all,
this time for profit
in hedge funds,
tax dodges.

Trespassers
will be prosecuted,
even in the 21st century,
except in Scotland, where
socialism
gave the right to roam.

At Risby, the big house
is an earthwork now,
garden terracing ridges
next to a silted-up lake.
Only the folly remains –
a eulogy to possession. ⁄⁄

Pebbles

At Spurn I stack your pebbles
and you begin a new journey.
Once stripped from a Swedish fjord,
larvikite was rolled in the icy grip
of glaciers: eroded, travelling
southwards in ice sheets across
Skagerrak and Dogger.

I love the reveal of your blue crystals
dampened by summer waves.
If I take you home
rain will imitate the effect,
and your schillerised plagioclase
will remind me of this walk
and my father's grave. ✍

Night Blight

Following the ancient road home
down the dip slope of The Wolds,
from Fridaythorpe to Wetwang.
The sky panoptic: stars, planets,
a diversity of heavenly bodies.

Any Parisi charioteers
would have seen more –
night-blight renders the visible invisible.

Sky-glow from distant cities brightens,
intrudes into darkness,
our folly a beacon illuminating all.

We see only hundreds out of thousands of stars
our ancestors knew by heart.
Charting night skies without their constellations. ⁂

Wressle Castle

Church towers, occasional trees erupt from flatlands.
A red-brick village hurries by, straight roads, hedgerows,
canals.
Not enough trees to keep us green.

Straight edges of concrete as stations rush by in a blur.
White-stoned Wressle Castle stands by the river,
reflecting past glories.

Once the Percys ruled the North, now it's the Tories.
Land which rolls out flat, reclaimed from lake,
shared amongst the rich.

Trespass a crime unforgiven by landowners
who possess the land and all its life.
They tax food, water, air

without a care.
I remember this was a country which taught equality
but no longer believes in it.

When royalty ruled from castles, people slaved;
now the parasites are rich,
preserving medieval England amongst the ruins. ⁄⁄

Drax

There are clouds tiled on the horizon
but they are not natural.
Birds wheel through gases
"within statutory limits".

The clouds around Drax form
when we make electricity,
steam from cooling towers,
nitrous oxides from the tallest chimney.

The proposition is, this doesn't matter,
the air will accept, absorb,
remain pure, blow pollution east,
but we're not sure.

Droplets of water condense
on particles of soot, salt, dust.
Concrete walls push out their vapours.
How much of this are we allowed?

The ocean of air belongs to all
to smell, to taste, to blow a kiss.
Why do we stand for this when
all we want to do is breathe? ⚓

East of Zero

East gets less each year. The curse of stupidity,
like Cnut forbidding high tide.

We protect vital assets scourging softer land south
to its fate in the grey North Sea.

East Riding – it marks final landfall
before the Greenwich meridian touches the North Pole.

Long-shore drift erodes Easington, Kilnsea,
ground to sediment deposited at Spurn.

Earth is scooped away by the Holderness Ord,
a wyrm of water uncoiling, twisting, making land sea again.

Zero is imagined – a construct for longitude.
In one hundred years nothing will be east of here

and our house, twelve miles from the coast,
will become littoral. ⁄⁄

Ravenser Odd

But this is December, no spring tides.
The bell sounds in alarm over the mudflats,
reminding me of villages long ago devoured by the sea.
The bell of Ravenser Odd is all that survives.
The town of the living dismantled,
the town of the dead reinterred
within earshot of the bell.
The sea shall have them all,
the sea will make short work of man's creation.
A revenge on Bollingbroke's treason.

Boulder clay removed tide by tide.
The storm eroded the slender promontory
creating an island of Spurn.
This too will wash away.
All our names will wash away,
taking the toil of labourers,
the cry of babies,
their mother's milk and all land's green.
To leave a pale sky and
a cold grey ocean to rumble against the strand. ∥

Punctual

Born the day Edward VII died,
Grandpa recalled the boating lake as marsh,
Zeppelins bombing Hull,
people dying on trams from Spanish flu.

The number 40 bus drew up,
one minute to cross the road
and Gran served tea on china plates
at 5.47pm.

He checked wrist with pocket watch –
an accountant's precision for units.
Only once tea wasn't ready and
Grandpa retired silently to the shed.

Attitudes change as hemlines rise.
Grandpa arrives home,
places his briefcase in the hall,
puts on an apron, turns to Fanny Craddock.

The fish pie, a little dry,
too much salt and butter in the mash
but Gran sits, sherry in hand.
Reads the manifesto for her new career. ⁄⁄

Listening to Waves

Winter's roar on a frosty night
would find me sitting on the sill
in an old cotton dressing gown,
lights off.
I would throw open the bedroom window
and listen to the sounds of the sea,
with the path of moonlight
paving the way a dream might take.

Go to sleep.
The door shifted and
I'd jump between winceyette sheets
as mother's arm eased the window closed.
She warned me of sirens
who make men weak
and mermaids who drown
the meek and good
unless you say your prayers.

Through the glass, the physics of
a wave's increasing asymmetry
transferred energy as sound.
How shifting gravity as the moon
waxes and wanes creates tides.

Scatter my ashes in the ocean,
let my atoms drift across the
wide, life-giving sea and maybe
I will feel fingers ripple through
amniotic fluid.
Hear new waves. ⁄⁄

Hull University Through Sleet

There are many more bricks here now,
less green, more grey matter
if I believe the adverts.
They even do a geology degree
like the one I obtained when
buildings were named for departments,
not those who splashed the cash.

Yet walking campus paths
brings excitement.
If I didn't see my reflection
I might be young and passionate –
a believer in equality and socialism.

A young man practising for age;
an older man returning
to better his prospects and what
could be better than the
top floor of The Brynmor Jones?
Here Larkin's ghost shuffles
and Hull is diminished to bricked grids
defying The Humber's bank. ⫻

RAF Hutton Cranswick

There is nothing here, which isn't strictly true –
a perimeter road separates
fields of wheat from peas and oilseed rape.
Out of range, cars reverberate on the A164.

Startled by propane cannon, birds bank –
anti-aircraft cannon long ago silenced.
Nothing in this farmland betrays its past
except that metalled perimeter road.

From here Polish pilots flew Spitfires –
Rodeos over France to defeat the Nazis,
308 Squadron (Krakow) one of many.
Few returned.

Some made it home, some lie under stone.
War ended.
You can return to your free country.
Churchill betrayed them.

Their homecoming was a bullet,
if they were lucky,
and an unmarked grave.
Stalin saw to that.

There is nothing here to commemorate.
History is written by the victors,
unsurprisingly kind to Churchill,
the author who forgot their sacrifice. ⟍

White Roses

When you celebrated my birth with a rose
you settled on Iceberg.
I have the greater choice as you are returned to earth:
Aimee Vibert, Pole Star, Saratoga,
Cloud or Iceberg floribunda.
I settled on Iceberg, remembering
your pruning shears deadheading,
the careful weeding and hoeing to keep your blossoms strong.
How they bloomed all June.
How they bloomed as you lay dying.
Now when Iceberg flowers I remember your smile,
your gammy leg, your style quite formal –
a tie for all occasions, whistling *Charmaine*
as you walked down Thearne Lane,
finally home to tend your roses. ⁄⁄

Eske

Wide skies watch over Eske,
undulations in pasture remain
where a main street clattered
to carts, beasts of burden,
children playing, chattering people.

Silenced, the village was silenced.
What was here is conjecture;
a market, a fair teeming with life?
All once sheltered by the River Hull
is nothing now.

We walk the banks talking,
taking isolation in our stride,
fears for family and friends
put aside as we take exercise
in our time of plague.

Lives damaged, torn
apart by absent lovers.
Bones are bones, they fertilise
this green and pleasant pasture.
Past or present, what becomes of us?
What indeed becomes of us? ⁄⁄

Kenley Reach

Cloud shadows chase the tidal surge upstream,
framed by green embankments.
Of the farm, only the first floor peered
above the levee, catching the river's gleam.

We broke from our chores as The Arctic Corsair
floated by on its maiden voyage.
The trawler dwarfed the roofline, flat fields
and the rich soil under the ploughshare.

Damp seeped into everything at Kenley Reach.
Rheumatic fever took my uncle, then a feud
deprived the family of fields and laid them waste,
so no birds sing and ghosts in silence preach. ⁄⁄

Thearne Hall

This grey brick building
punctuates my early memories
when we expected to own land.
Now we live at the Wold's edge
and cycle here – keeping fit.

The rooks *kraa* their praise,
build their nests high this year,
they *craw* without care,
rob twigs to make their own nest.
One crow, many rooks, Grandad said.

He mentioned sundry things in his will
but not the farm, no land received.
How the brothers were deceived.
I would never have made a farmer's son,
retching when I entered the dairy.

I listen to rooks, high in their ash trees,
their parliament a raucous clamour.
I take off my cap and realise that's
the action Grandad made to shield his eyes,
watching rooks, glad to be alive. ⁄⁄

High Eske

There is nothing protecting us
from this raw north-westerly,
no windbreak between us
and the far High Wold.

This river is stealthy,
canoes and paddle-boarders
use the tide flowing silently
to reach their destination.

Winter is in the teasel,
dry whispering reeds –
last gasps of so many
taken by this woeful season.

Still frost, still blue –
a landscape of reflections
stretched thin like the river
restrained by muddy banks.

This is our daily walk
squelching along well-trodden paths.
When will we be free to fly noisily
like geese in close formation? ⁄⁄

Quiet Flows the Hull

I can see Beverley Minster across the ings.
Towers of magnesian limestone
glimpsed between trees across
flatlands ancestors tilled.

Magnified through air's prism,
Great John chimes the hour
as it has since 1901.
Heard by four generations, now gone.

No place a shadow can hide
under the sun, where the Hull flows
silver, sometimes sapphire,
often grey under a sodden sky.

Old willows feel the tug of tides,
roots securing the banks, holding fast.
Our roots secure, becoming entwined
with each ebb and flow of the river.

The carillon's peel carried east
across the ings. A song ancestors heard
as they tilled these fields, toiled,
aware of their here, their now. ⁄⁄

Wincolmlee

Wincolmlee is married to the river,
matching meander to embankment,
pretending not to notice its muddy
effluent marking the limit.

When we walked along Wincolmlee to
The Whale Bone, with smoke cascading
from its fire, from cigarettes, from pipes,
I'd sit in the corner drinking shandy –
grandpa leaned against the bar talking business.

Later, cameras poised,
I saw only the sink and swell of the river,
the decaying fabric of this once great port;
rotting brickwork, silent chimneys all
redundant like Scott Street Bridge.

Grandpa took photos of people:
a man fishing by a rusting cleat,
a woman in a headscarf,
a tramp sleeping against a gravestone
chiselled with our surname.

Wincolmlee ends where mud
sucks in trollies, the foolhardy,
the remains of our days,
preserving discarded truths
in a twice daily reveal. ⁄⁄

Gran's Cloche Hat

Gran would not be seen without a hat:
church, shopping, a doctor's appointment,
walking her poodle in East Park.
To go without a hat would be
beyond the pale, as she was fond of saying.

Her favourite – a simple cloche,
black felt, ennobled by three feathers,
peacock eyes – crescents of blue –
unfathomable black. Gran extolled
peacocks as the symbol of royalty.

She had aspirations. Hats highlighted status.
I held the poodle's lead, Gran walked beside,
Good morning, for owners of pedigree dogs,
never a word for mongrels.
Peacocks in the park fanned their tails,

screamed their calls, rattled in courtship.
We watched for ages. So many photos
we possess of 1960s peacocks, their beauty
frozen in display; one hundred eyes that
mock the dead trio on Gran's black hat. ⟋

Swans at East Park

Mute swans mate for life like you and I.
They glide the summer waters
as we walk by.
Silent in their thoughts, they never sing
until the call of death creates a hymn.
They swim gracefully like an angel might,
feathers preened 'til water tight.
They navigate the sinuous curves of
East Park's lake
as children erupt from the academy's gate
to swear and smoke.
We look at each other and walk on in silence
secure in our alliance like the swans,
content to tread the sinuous curves of
East Park's lake. ⁄⁄

The Splash Boat

Not one, not two, not three, not four
but five generations awestruck by the gravity
of this mechanism.
To queue and climb the steps.
We choose our seat and wait with trepidation
between heartbeats.
Movement slowly accelerates,
the roar of wood on rail accumulates
and screaming punctuates
descent
until the nose plunges and the plume of water
arcs and thrills
drop by drop
onto us,
our neighbours,
mums and dads,
clandestine lovers.
Finally the vessel judders.
The splash boat hauled to home by jute,
we disembark
to watch the next crew
ride the water chute. ⁄⁄

Wobbly

The love which once was there
doesn't apply today.
A sleepless night,
one of many,
so reluctantly,
with stinging eyes,
we don scarves, coats, hats
and push the daughter
whose love has squeezed between us
to the park.
She doesn't sleep.
She points at dogs,
pretends to bark,
then by the big enclosure says,
"Look! A wobbly."

A wallaby.
She giggles with delight
watching the marsupial's white fur,
the way it hops
or waits without a care.
For once our daughter's silent.
I look again, she's fast asleep.
Quietly we turn around and push for home
and dream of sleep ourselves or, not content with one,
to contemplate the pleasure of another.
A brother? ⁄⁄

Walling Fen

Looking out over Brantingham
and beyond to the plain,
rivers become an inland sea as
Trent and Ouse converge on Humber.

This view looks permanent,
distant embankments developed as
generations toiled to hold back floods
and keep land below sea-level above water.

Parisi ancestors would have seen
a tidal lake, swamps, sand banks,
fish and fowl for the plate,
boats trading between tribes.

A human life is too short
to encompass change,
when we believe we have tamed the land
and made it a possession. ⁄⁄

Burton Fleming

Rustling leaves in the churchyard,
seasoned like parchment,
trees dwarfing St Cuthbert's
where saplings sprout
from the squat tower
with roots nearer heaven.

On the landscape,
older by far is Willie Howe,
where the breeze chants of winters
yet to come.
November leaves swirl and
birdsong accompanies the wind's
fall through the valley.

The winterbourne stream
springs to life,
a dry valley exhaling water
and chalk bones surrendered by the soil
anchor roots of new life. ⁂

Door, Wharram-le-Street

The year Edward the Confessor's head
first appeared on coins,
stones were quarried, carried,
dressed or carved,
set one upon another
to make this doorway.

Behind this tall, narrow door
the mystery of
ceremonies held in half-light
for half-believers,
be they Saxon or Viking,
living a fragile peace.

A sandstone doorway
which welcomed all
until the squire wanted a porch.
The original walled up.
Behold! The new entrance
with its aspirations.

We are still divided,
half believers in equality
living a fragile peace.
All doors now barred,
the year Elizabeth the second's head
last appeared on a coin. ⁄⁄

Belshazzar's Feast

The writing is on the wall
but not enough people read the words
or hear the message.
The feast continues unabated:
exotic foods flown from around the world,
Antipodean wines, rare flesh on which to dine
and standing decked in polyester from crude oil,
and cotton from the toil of hungry children,
Belshazzar stands immune from everything.
He has more than enough money to feed the poor.
The world has not enough, yet he wants more:
more heat, more light, more meat,
more to delight the senses,
he senses the writing's on the wall,
knows he cannot have it all and continue.
He'd like to save the world but cannot save himself
without air he cannot breathe,
without water what use is wealth?
So he returns to feast –
the writing still on the wall,
ignored by many
and by others never read at all. ⁄

John Harrison

Miscalculation of longitude caused
the British fleet to sink off The Scilly Islands.

After the drownings, a prize was offered:
John Harrison rose to the challenge.

It was simply a matter of time:
knowing it precisely at Greenwich
whilst aboard ship anywhere in the world.

His task, designing a chronometer which kept
the seconds with every pitch and yaw,
come rain or shine, heat or cold.

John Harrison dreamed in clockwork,
moved vertical cogs horizontal,
each solution, each advance saving time, saving lives.

Grasshopper escapement, brass fusée, wooden cogs,
remontoire, a jewelled going train,

always miniaturising until a pocket watch
ran trials across the Atlantic.

Here at the prime meridian where seconds linger
I can only wonder how with five ticks per second

he solved the problem of longitude,
charting the way for all to stay on course. ⁄⁄

Sea of Hull

Beyond the checkpoint.
I queued to register,
received an empty plastic bag
labelled B3.
Queued for body paint
marvelling at the number and diversity
of people – all talking.

Just after 4 with a red dawn,
Spencer ordered us to strip and paint our bodies,
giving our skin a new colour –
helping hands daubed backs
and I became turquoise.
Nudity made us equal:
as we walked, colours mixed,
leaving footprints in shades of blue until
three thousand people filled The Rose Bowl.
My backside made it onto Sky News!

The unyielding tarmac of Alfred Gelder Street
was bitterly cold, so when the breeze blew
an *ooo* emanated from the crowd.
Spencer called his assistant –
"St*eee*ve," mimicked through the ranks.
A Mexican Wave helped prevent shivering.
A joke about a red light broke the ice
before we were marshalled into colours
for the next take.

We surrounded an eminent Victorian's statue:
our nakedness a stark contrast to his baronial robes.
Our final photo found us crammed on
Scale Lane bridge.
"That's a cut!"
A round of applause. Cheers!

Four of the coldest July hours but we'd made it!
A Sea of Hull reaching out the
hand of friendship in shades of blue. ✍

Wolds

Raindrops fall on the windscreen
and are swept away.
Raindrops fall greeting another day.
Hills run out of energy
before the flatlands where
rubble fields
submit to clay-rich Holderness.
Photographs do not
flatter this landscape;
it appears flat beneath
skies of any hue.
The gentle sweep of the wold top
deceptively hides dry valleys.
Soils drift downhill, leaving summits
boned with chalk.
Skeletal fingers of ancestors
claw their way from barrows
into daylight.

Raindrops fall on the windscreen
to leave an indecipherable message
which is swept away.
Rain chatters on the windscreen
before being swept away.
The radial wipe erases the past
with mesmerising certainty.
Grey clouds meet damp chalk,
tarmac, road spray
landing on the windscreen –
swept away.
Raindrops defy gravity,
their patterns roll uphill –
wind resistance versus speed.

Raindrops fall on the windscreen
and are swept away.
The work of ancestral labourers,
swept away.
Climb eight hundred feet to
watch rain turn to snow from
cloud filled skies.
We talk of love
leave indecipherable messages,
swept away.
Our generation
grows older as another develops.
Driving across the wolds –
a landscape at once ancient
and modern – unsung like hymns.

A patch of blue opening
as the wolds diminish.
Blue sky, forget-me-nots at the verge –
a swathe of colour as monotones
give way to sunlight.
Landscape stretched
as far as the sea.
Life giving way to life –
To our daughter, a daughter.
Once I was the foundation of
the family tree
now two generations beyond support me. ⁄⁄

Port Mulgrave

Disconnected, inaccessible,
this hamlet of flotsam and jetsam,
formed partly from sea's gifts,
the remainder descended precipitous cliffs.

Steps fly on visiting air,
bent iron frames might dare me to descend
but January's storm ripped half away,
now only fishermen brave the climb.

Shale juxtaposed against a wild fantastic sea
where seals breed, whales become beached.
A crack! Before a tumbling melange
of cliff threatens to bury these shacks.

People imagine merfolk
copulating on the strand amongst our waste.
Their moans congruous with flowing spume,
bellies full of microplastic from their diet of fish.

I long to connect with such inaccessible places,
to search further between rocks for fossils –
the memorabilia of a real Jurassic Park.
Evidence to counter creationism.

Blue sky, blue sea,
breakwater churning waves,
Iron mining a memory not quite as distant
as the tropical oceans which laid down these rocks. //

Snowglobe

Inside the snow globe
all is beautiful if you hold the scene still.
People listen to a brass band,
medleys of Arthur Gilbert with
solos on horn, trumpet, euphonium
under the watch of Queen Victoria.

Held in limbo for the shake of a hand,
a child's delight
in upending everything –
memories, mere dust-motes
layer over the bandstand ensuring
perfection is obscured by decay.

Ghosts are gathering today,
flapping deckchairs under overcast skies.
People queue for ice-creams whilst
medleys of Luigi Denza are accompanied by
solos on tuba, trombone, cornet.
Everything is surface inside a snow globe.

Shake, watch the transformation –
instantaneous entropy settling
into a perfect scene, everything
clean like Mamma says it should be.
A snow globe contains an element of truth
preserved only when disturbed. ⁄⁄

Lockdown Quartet

Sylvia

I rattle,
my schedule of pills,
empty rooms filled with framed memories.
The telephone echoes
and if my finger joints unlock, I answer.
Meals slip by an hour or
slip by uneaten but
every morning at eleven,
my walking frame and I
make it to a seat by the door.
If it's warm, my tea grows cold
as we talk out an hour.

Barbara, Rob, Audrey, Jean,
all at our doors – two metres apart.
We chat – what's happened across the quad?
And if there is a god, typical man,
he's not listening.
The couple upstairs have the virus:
we look up into their silence.
Makes you wonder
how long we have to go
before carers do their rounds
without face shields, masks,
nothing except devotion to their tasks.

Brenda

In lockdown, I alternate walking and cycling,
I've walked The Westwood so often
I know every lump and bump,
barrow and hollow as if it was my own body.

If the weather's bad we *YouTube* an exercise class,
I say we...
my husband's uncoordinated,
he makes me laugh attempting the grapevine,
bunny hop, cha-cha-cha...
complaining his hips ache.
Hips don't lie when you're ageing.

Cycling wins for Wold views:
uphill and home or downhill and home?
All this is killing time,
keeping us fit but killing time.
Spring turns – April's gone,
May's revealed,
and it's such a long time
since I hugged our daughter:
when will I be able to
cuddle our grand-daughter again?

Eleanor

How many days?
Let me count them:
full-time furlough,
full-time child care,
but this is different
caring for my four year old
and bump within.
I leave the house to walk our dog.
I leave the house for scans
and send ultrasound photos

to relatives around the world.
Next street, next city, next country –
distance doesn't matter,
I'm the one isolating.

How many weeks?
Let me count them.
New life, new hope, they say.
I'm nervous of each brush with humanity,
are they carriers?
I am eager for each brush with humanity,
even at two metres –
but it's not just me to consider
when there's this new life within.

Amelia

We wash our hands
because of germs.
We stay apart
because of germs.
We stand apart
because of germs.
I don't see friends
because of germs.
No swings
no slides
because of germs.
No grandma,
grandpa
because of germs.
Pretend to hug
because of germs.
Phone and facetime
because of germs.
Happy times with
YouTube ballet,
baking,

dog-walking,
cycling,
crafts and painting,
trampoline;
if it's warm,
the paddling pool,
swingball.
Happy days. ⁄⁄

The Modifications of Clouds

We are all victims of clouds;
the unexpected shower,
an unannounced kiss in the shelter.
Cumulonimbus possess the anvil
to echo my heartbeat in thunder
when I'm close to you.
Warm air holds more water:
a warm heart holds more love.

A cloud's secret –
water is eternally recycled
as vapour, rain, hail, snow,
each molecule has seen it all:
the embrace of lovers through time,
the dawn chorus of birds
before their feathers evolved.
Rain on silent Devonian plains,
seas where trilobites swam.
Through the water cycle
we see the same molecules
devoted to the Earth,
a true repeater of births.
Cirrus, stratus, cumulus,
layers in the ocean of air
which embraces us all –
as we embrace in the shelter,
innocent victims of clouds. ⟋

Bubbles

Bubbles are a water sandwich
of hydrophilic heads and
hydrophobic tails.

As water evaporates,
the distance between soap layers
decreases causing iridescence.

Spheres are the smallest shape
for the volume of air, while
glycerine slows evaporation.

None of which conveys the joy
my granddaughter has
on sunny days, for bubbles.

Gladly I oblige:
a four year old and grandpa
both enjoy, enthuse and play

with fragile bubbles which rise
into the sky. Blow into the wand,
let the breeze take them
and their upside-down reflections. ⁄⁄

Spectre of the Brocken

I've only once possessed a halo –
on the summit of a mountain
my shadow cast like a shroud
onto mist, sunlight diffracted
into a rainbow round my head.
My own personal nimbus.

It set me thinking about the sky –
how it's blue and why
light scatters in the air from
molecules of oxygen and nitrogen.
Their interference a Rayleigh scattering
of shorter wavelength blues and a smattering
of violet.
Does the sea reflect the sky?
Or sky the sea and does it matter?
Is the whiteness of the sun simply Mie scatter?

I've only once possessed a halo –
on the summit of a mountain
my shadow was cast like an angel
but no one else would ever see it. ⁄⁄

Wind

Wind,
wrap your arms around me;
dance whilst I breathe;
tousle my hair.
At the summit I wait for your caress,
soft and warm like a lover in summer's heat,
angry like a spurned wife through winter's storms.
You follow me to distant lands,
so as I lie somnolent on a foreign beach
you blow sand into the pages of my book.
Your fingers reaching out,
touching but never waiting to be held.
I have my words for you, wind:
Breeze, squall, gust, gale,
you puff of air, you draft, you waft,
the cunning zephyr of my laments,
a chatterer of leaves to counter my laughter.
You are the motion of air,
an anticyclone wrapped round low pressure,
which I'll always need to breathe. ⁄⁄

Allan-Williams Turret

Today I can see for miles –
nothing between me and the horizon
except a cold wind drawn from Svalbard.
Nothing beyond salt marsh.
From here it's impossible to chart Blakeney Channel
distracted by the dive of marsh harriers amongst reeds.
A watch house on the point awaits high tide, storm,
but here amongst water's malaise, the bittern's croak
remains unfathomable.
Leave this edge of Norfolk to the ways of birds:
the lost language of terns,
herons silently dispatching elver,
depriving them of distant seas.
Where amongst this mudflat
does something become nothing?
Where samphire grows or skylarks sing
or the breeze whips up a sting?
Or in slow rusting of an Allan-Williams Turret,
its panorama sinking into turgid mire? //

Beinn Gharbh

Rough mountain, how I long to be young again
beneath your Torridonian sandstone bluffs.
My first field mapping was here and I felt failure.
I refused to climb down to Doire Daimh when
my partner suggested it. Snow showers, ice,
a fear of heights all made me say *no*.
In the debrief, I confused basic and ultrabasic dykes.
Weather and lack of knowledge had conspired against me.
I believed I was experienced outdoors but hours
later I knew I was a dreamer, I watched
clouds reflect in Loch Assynt, imagined
Ardvreck Castle's history – how Covenanters briefly won.
I had my geological map graded a low second.
There is unfinished business here – I need to go back. ⁄⁄

Field Trip

A class of students climbing over slag heaps,
waterproof trousers, kagoules,
rain dripping off noses, fogging glasses.
For God's sake no one ask any questions
or we'll be here forever. (It feels like forever.)
Tungsten, lead, copper, arsenic ores
but only gangue litters the surface now.
We rip through it to reveal more dirt.

Mineral veins formed when hot magma cooled,
differentiated, permeated layers.
Looking up, the fell
following veins hacked out by mining,
an arterial excision, extracting ores.

Damp permeates everything,
chill sets in as we descend ancient gabbros
darker than our moods.
Industry needs tungsten, lead, copper, arsenic,
that's why we undergraduates were here –
to learn how to rob a planet of its riches,
spoil a mountain of its beauty.
Thankfully, I never had a chance.
No poet ever looted a planet
or ever saved one. ⁄⁄

I Juggy

Here is where hiding began:
my arrival at headquarters,
first job after graduating.
Passport, suitcase carried under
an arm aching from vaccinations:
Hep A, typhoid, yellow fever.

There's a position on our land-based
seismic survey, Warrington.
Interesting work on Irlam Bog.
Here's a train ticket, report to Barry
at The King's Head this evening.

I've had all the vaccinations for Brazil.
Change of plan – this is the place for real men.
I felt less real by the second
but made it second class to Warrington.
Mercifully, station to hotel was a short walk.

I started as a juggy – a geophone stomper –
helping reveal what lies beneath the earth.
All day I had to be someone I was not;
a man who swore, smoked, spat.
JB said, *every hole drilled was filled,*
that's the nature of holes, they need something
warm inside them, dynamite, my cock!
I gave a nervous laugh.
The hiding continued.
I wanted to be someone I was not,
to follow in the footsteps of Hardy.
I was caught reading his poetry.
Kiss me! Kiss me!
Wrong Hardy.
No one listened, too busy laughing.

What lies beneath the earth
can be revealed by geophysics.
What lies beneath the skin of a man
is hidden forever.
Expectations –
Barry gave friendly advice:
You've got to adapt, fit in,
Drink, swear, indulge in sin.

A juggy – a geophone stomper –
boots clagged with mud and clay.
Lunch: fish, chips 'n' peas.
An afternoon of mind-numbing tedium;
line check, line break,
line telephone to control,
batteries replaced,
line ready.

Ten pounds of dynamite explode.
Vibrations entering the earth
revealing what lies beneath.
Finally the signal goes up.
Collect everything in.

It's growing dark, getting cold,
joints and muscles ache.
Men stomp by, muttering profanities.
This is no place to discuss humanity
or look at Venus rising in the sky,
see shadows through a poet's eyes.

My boots grow heavier,
arms and shoulders hurt carrying
geophone pins.
Every item counted in.
At seven released from purgatory,
offered fish, chips 'n' peas –
day one of being a juggy. ⧷

Hundale Point

Standing at Hundale Point
on the wave-cut platform,
teams of keen geologists
measured paleo currents,
orientation of fossils, worm casts
preserved in Jurassic sediments.
A final field trip before graduation.

Forty years later I'm here again,
the wave-cut platform empty,
fossils still visible
preserving that moment
when sea levels rose and
sediments smothered.

Faces staring from this graduation photo:
1981's professors always seemed old
but friends who never made 60?
Draw a line through the faces
of those no longer here,
return the photo to its drawer
and let it wait. ✐

Gowbarrow Fell

Molecules of water tumble over High Force,
under the bridge, corkscrewing through Aira Force
where harder rock resists erosion,
creating a waterfall.

One day some of these billions of molecules
will make it back to Gowbarrow Fell,
falling as rain slaking parched peat,
collecting in idle bogs, where cotton grass nods.

Flowers of every hue: blue orchid, pink herb robert,
purple thyme, abundant yellows punctuate our hike
down from the peak, following the contours,
revealing ever unfolding panoramas of lake and hills.

Photos contain some things the eye cannot retain,
light playing on Place Fell, mottling its rolling greens,
brightening ancient igneous rocks spewed from volcanoes,
harder than the ancient bedrock.

Flows of andesitic lava aren't credited with much:
an eruption 480 million years ago
is now the heart of this fell, not beating, just here
as background in this selfie celebrating the peak. ⁄⁄

The Hayburn Wyke Plant Bed

A long time ago –
one hundred and seventy million years approximately,
the place that would become here
was a lush delta feeding an ancient sea.

Conifers, ferns, liverworts and ginkgo
washed down in floods, came to rest
and by a miracle of preservation –
fossilised in this plant bed.

Imprints of delicate leaves
veined and ribbed,
bark textures, horsetail roots –
all evidence of warm littoral summers.

Distant descendants cling to these cliffs,
temperate oaks shadow the geology,
their hopes for immortality
too soon granted by erosion. ⟋

Ted Harben

Sometimes I'd turn up unannounced
with my latest poem
which Ted would read,
take off his glasses, suck the temple tip,
reflect.

Erudition – a favourite word,
accessibility – no place for the absurd.
Each week the Scarborough News
carried his verses of germane muse.

He gave me an abiding love of
Eliot, Spender, Auden, Graves –
The greats of his pre-war youth
before military service changed all.

Never without a knitted tank top
and green cord jacket.
His tie a Windsor knot but
asserted by a simple pin of course!

He never made a scene or allowed a racket
but bore the creed of 70s creativity.
Took school trips to Stratford
to watch *the greats*.

I remember he once said I'd make a poet.
He loved the signed edition sent although it
didn't quite match his aspirations –
too much free verse.

I last met him cycling through town.
He stopped, saw my daughter,
exclaimed, "My God! You've bred!"
Smiled at his acerbic joke,
shook my hand warmly.
"Never give up on dreams," he said. ⁄⁄

Acknowledgements

The following poems have been published in literary magazines and collections:

Ravenser Old: *The Algebra of Owls*
Kenley Reach: *Leeds Lieder Festival* (music by John Sturt)
Listening to Waves: *Dream Catcher Issue 37*
Walling Fen: *Dream Catcher Issue 39 & High Wolds Poetry Festival Anthology #1*
Eske: *High Wolds Poetry Festival Anthology #2*
East of Zero: *The Poetry Village, Consilience #4*
Belshazzar's Feast: *Dreich #9*
Riding the Riding: *Spelt #1*
Receiver of Wreck: *Orbis #194*
Sylvia: *Geography is Irrelevant*
Still Life with Skylark: *Geography is Irrelevant / Summer Anywhere*
Swans at East Park: *Avocet*
Modifications of Clouds: *Dream Catcher Issue 35*
Bubbles: *Gentian #8 Reflections*
Quiet Flows the Hull: *The York Literary Review*
Wind: *Dream Catcher Issue 33*
John Harrison, Gentleman: *Consilience #10 Measurement Issue*
Hundale Point: *192 Magazine#3*

Other anthologies and collections available from Stairwell Books

For further information please contact rose@stairwellbooks.com
www.stairwellbooks.co.uk
@stairwellbooks